Brian Batchelor

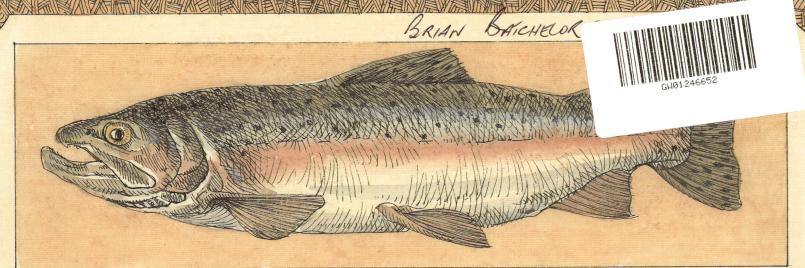

Rainbow Trout (Salmo gairdnerii).

Brown Trout (Salmo trutta)

Copyright © 1990 Jim Ayers
Copyright © 1990 David Bateman Ltd.

First published in 1990 by
David Bateman Ltd.
'Golden Heights', 32-34 View Road, Glenfield,
Auckland, New Zealand.

ISBN 1-86953-002-0

All rights reserved. No part of this publication may be reproduced or transmitted in any form or by any means without the permission of the publishers.

Printed in Hong Kong by Colorcraft.

Dedicated to all fishermen, who by turning these pages, would like to relive the joys and sorrows of past fishing adventures.

Jim R Ayers

Date	Water Fished	Flies	Weather	Fish Caught
29/8/00	Tauranga Taupo Crescent Car Park afternoon	Weighted orange Muppet	Fine after rain, water cloudy.	1 x 2.5lb fresh run hen 1 x 2lb jack lost another 2
30/8/00	Tauranga Taupo nine pool early morning Noted 4 fisherman on the next pool below from true left bank were having good success.	Weighted orange Muppet	Fine water clearing	1 x 3½lb fresh run hen 1 x 4lb fresh run jack lost 2

Remarks

Date	Water Fished	Flies	Weather	Fish Caught

Remarks:

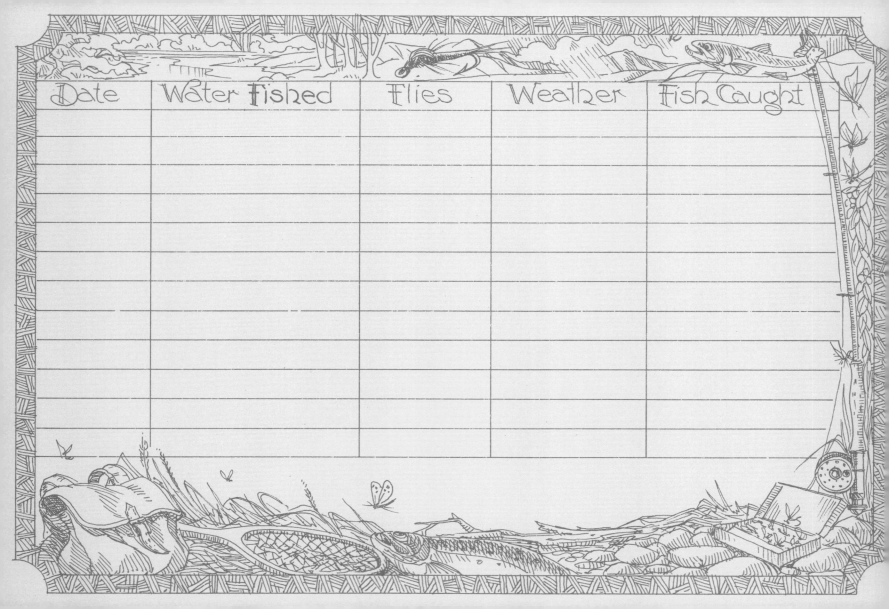

Date	Water Fished	Flies	Weather	Fish Caught

Remarks

Remarks:

Date	Water Fished	Flies	Weather	Fish Caught

Remarks

Remarks:

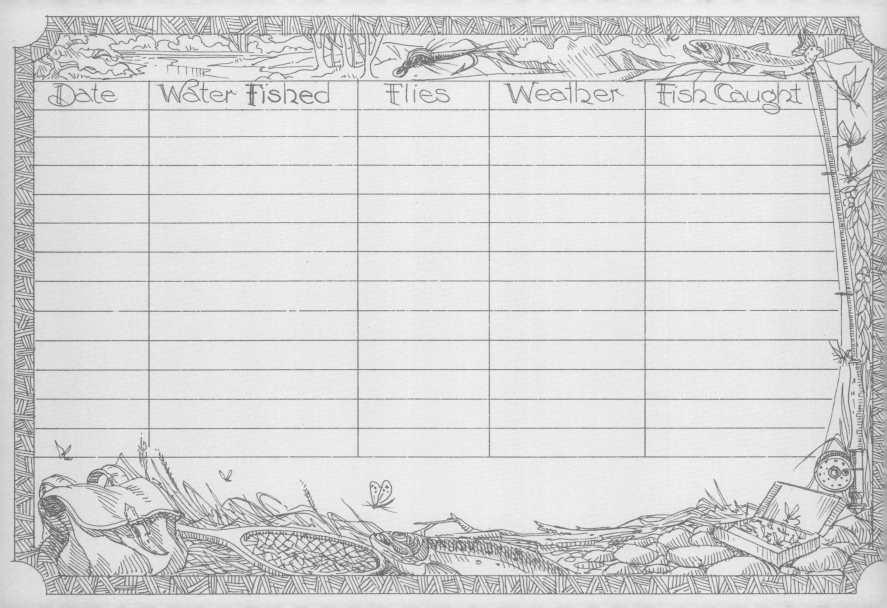

Remarks

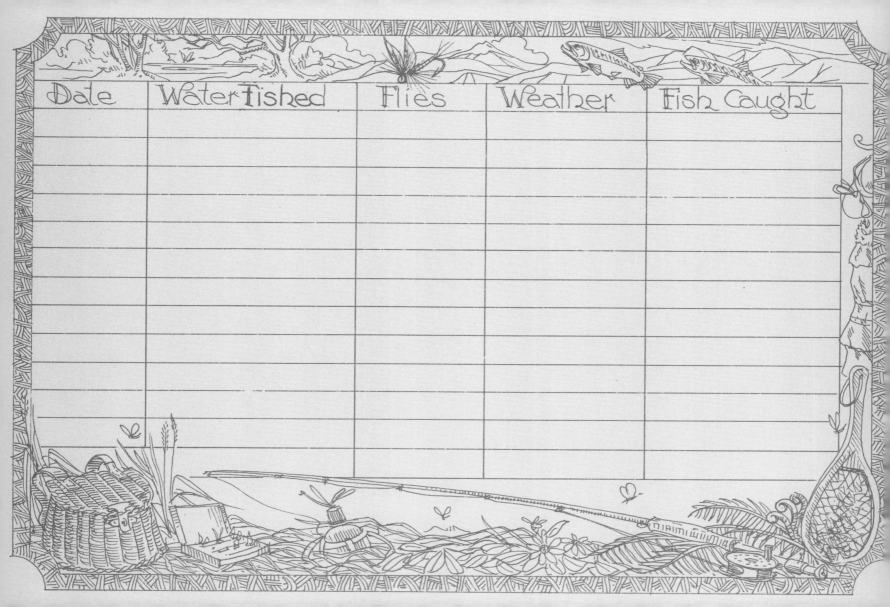

Date	Water Fished	Flies	Weather	Fish Caught

Remarks:

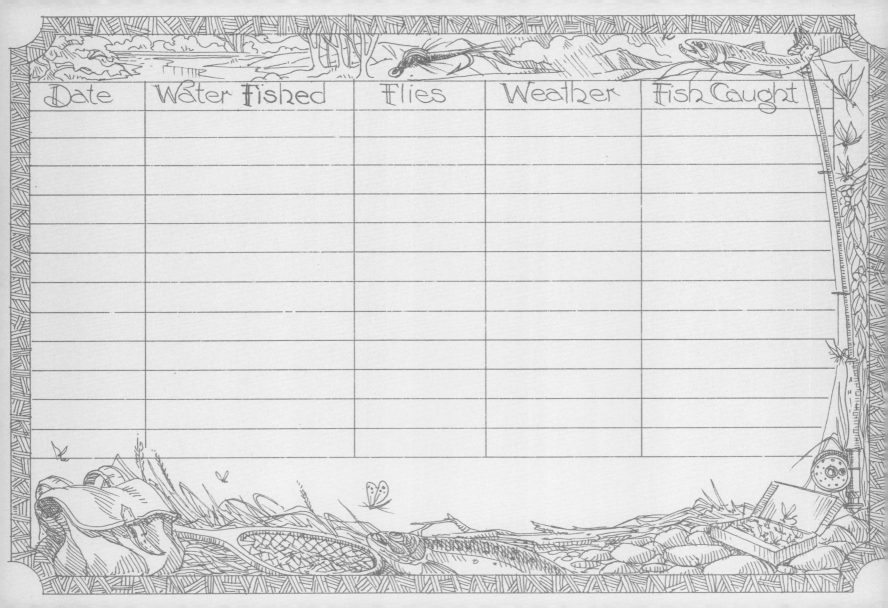

Remarks

Date	Water Fished	Flies	Weather	Fish Caught

Remarks:

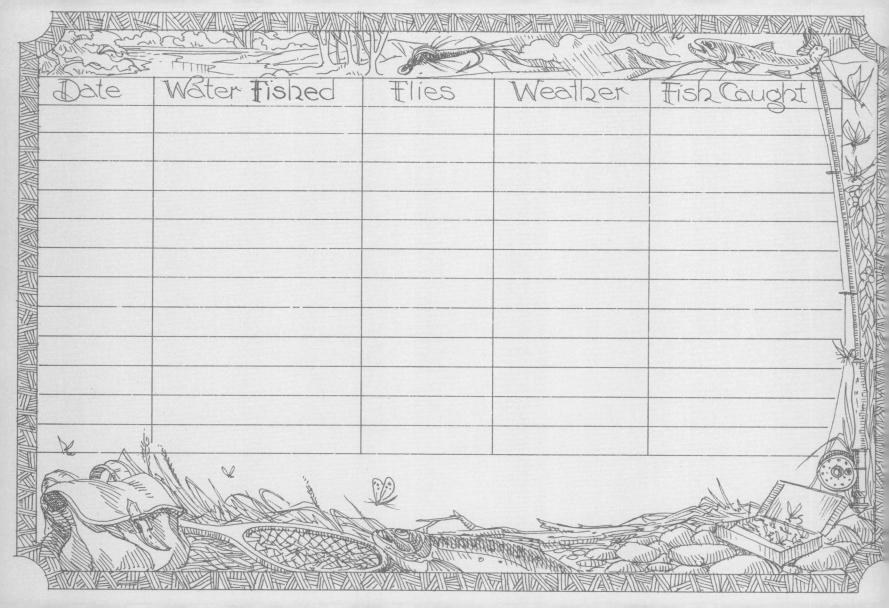

Date	Water Fished	Flies	Weather	Fish Caught

Remarks:

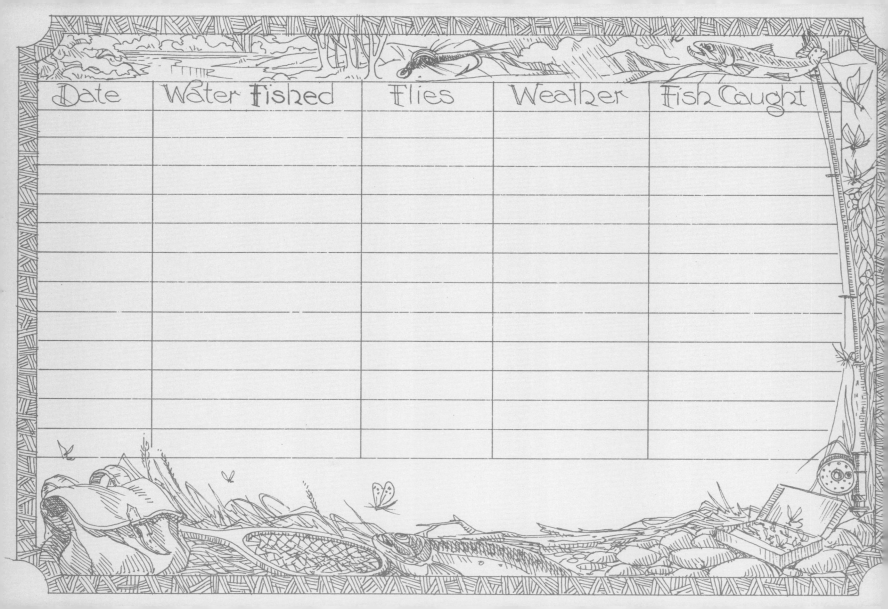

Date	Water Fished	Flies	Weather	Fish Caught

Remarks

Date	Water Fished	Flies	Weather	Fish Caught

Remarks:

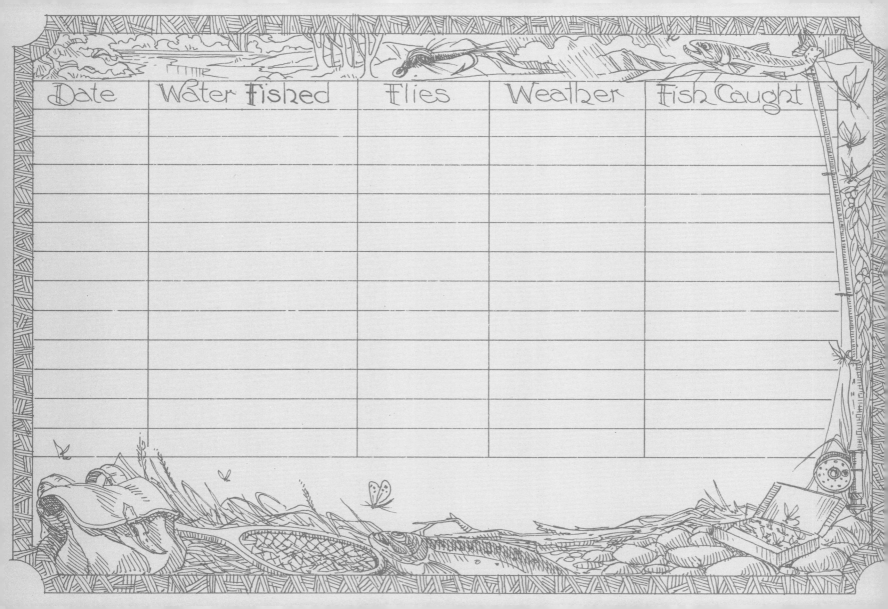

Remarks:

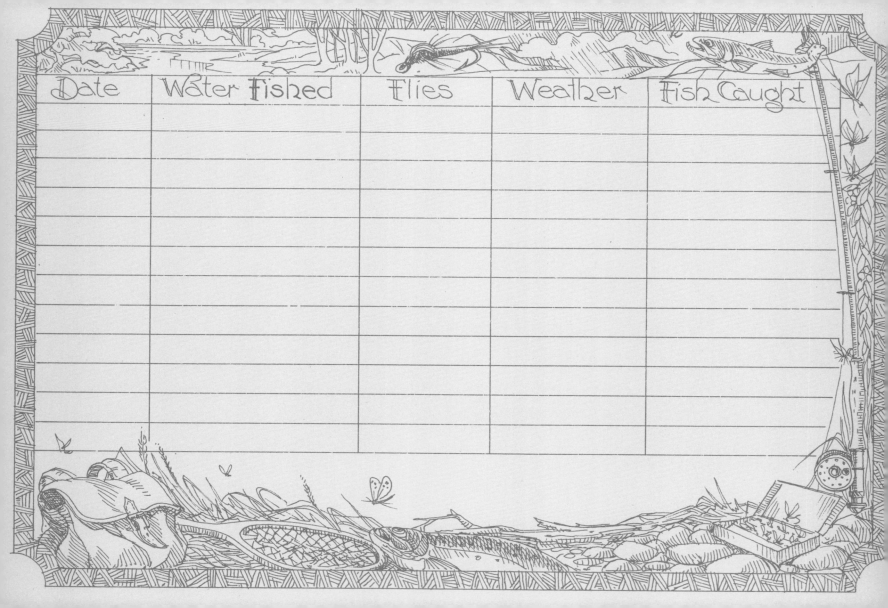

Remarks

Date	Water Fished	Flies	Weather	Fish Caught

Remarks:

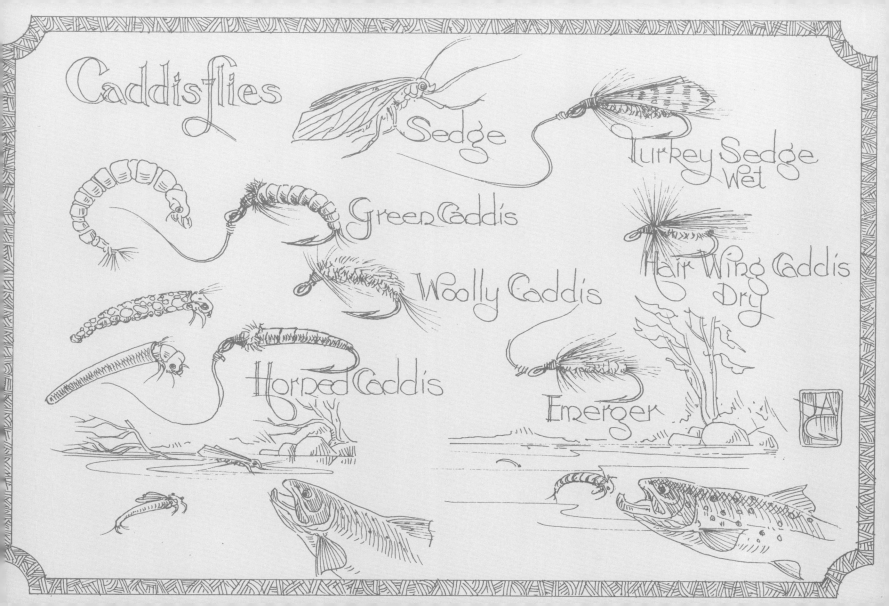

Summary of a Season 19____

Rainbows	Number	Salmon	Number
Hens			
Jacks			
Total		Total	
Browns		Others	
Hens			
Jacks			
Total			

Heaviest Fish: _____

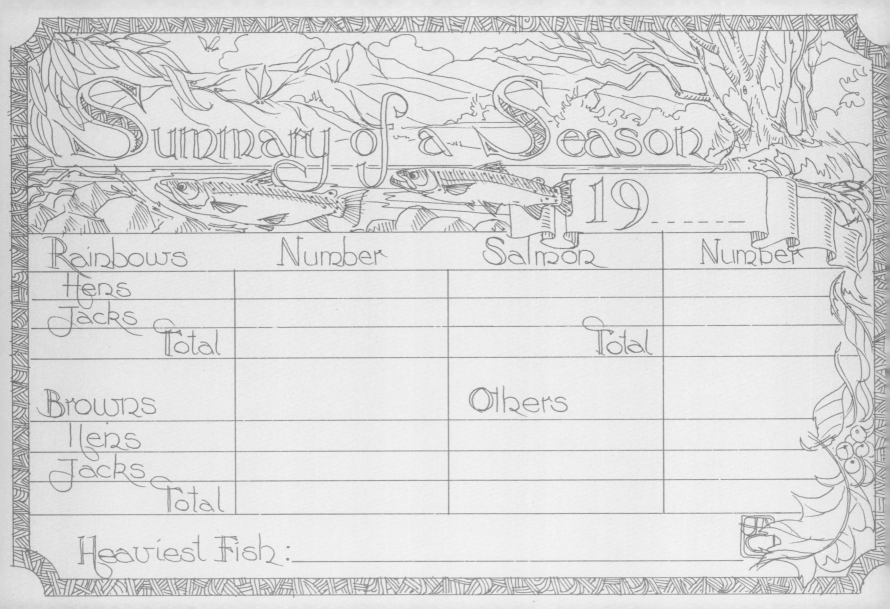

Addresses

Name	Address	Phone

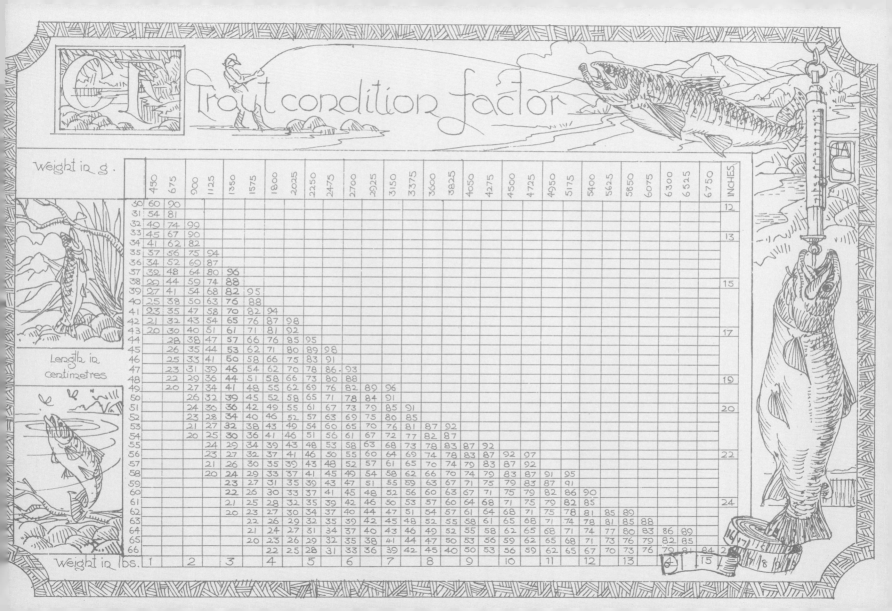

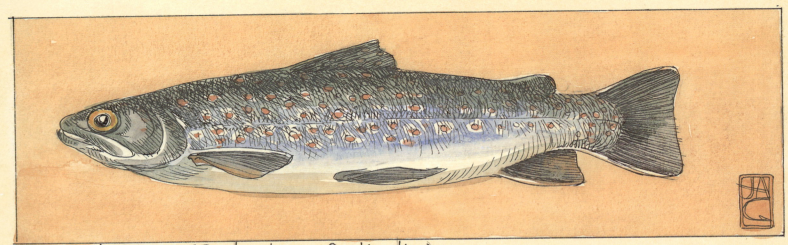

Brook Char (Salvelinus fontinalis)

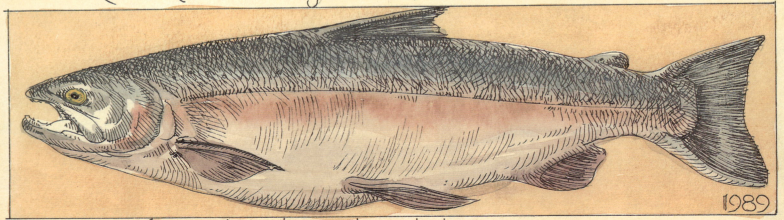

Salmon (Oncorhynchus tshawytscha)